How to Analyze the Works of

VIRGINIA
WOOLF

by Rosa Boshier

ABDO
Publishing Company

Essential Critiques

How to Analyze the Works of

VIRGINIA
WOOLF

by Rosa Boshier

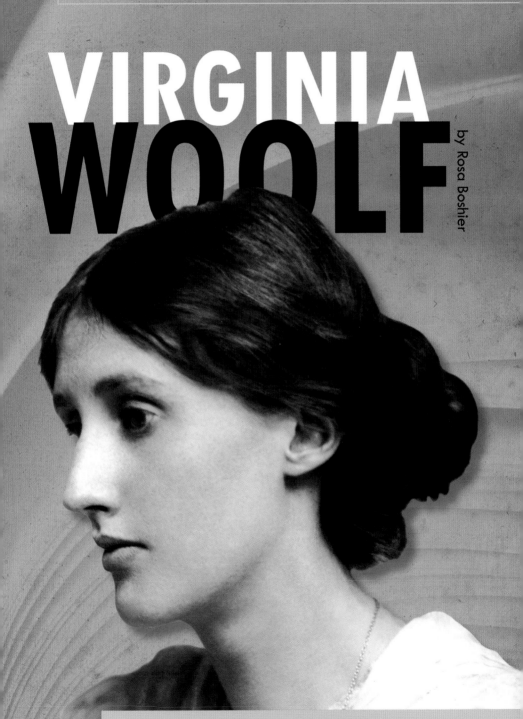

Content Consultant: Vara Neverow
Professor of English and Women's Studies, Southern Connecticut State University

Credits

Published by ABDO Publishing Company, PO Box 398166, Minneapolis, MN 55439. Copyright © 2013 by Abdo Consulting Group, Inc. International copyrights reserved in all countries. No part of this book may be reproduced in any form without written permission from the publisher. The Essential Library™ is a trademark and logo of ABDO Publishing Company.

Printed in the United States of America,
North Mankato, Minnesota
052012
092012

 THIS BOOK CONTAINS AT LEAST 10% RECYCLED MATERIALS.

Editor: Lauren Coss
Series Designer: Marie Tupy

Library of Congress Cataloging-in-Publication Data
Boshier, Rosa.
 How to analyze the works of Virginia Woolf / Rosa Boshier.
   p. cm. -- (Essential critiques)
 Includes bibliographical references.
 ISBN 978-1-61783-459-2
 1. Woolf, Virginia, 1882-1941--Criticism and interpretation--Juvenile literature.
I. Title.
 PR6045.O72Z56146 2013
 823'.912--dc23
                                        2012016734

Table of Contents

1

Introduction to Critiques

What Is Critical Theory?

What do you usually do when you read a book? You probably absorb the specific language style of the book. You learn about the characters as they are developed through thoughts, dialogue, and other interactions. You may like or dislike a character more than others. You might be drawn in by the plot of the book, eager to find out what happens at the end. Yet these are only a few of many possible ways of understanding and appreciating a book. What if you are interested in delving more deeply? You might want to learn more about the author and how his or her personal background is reflected in the book. Or you might want to examine what the book says about society—how it depicts the roles of

The end.

women and minorities, for example. If so, you have entered the realm of critical theory.

Critical theory helps you learn how various works of art, literature, music, theater, film, and other endeavors either support or challenge the way society behaves. Critical theory is the evaluation and interpretation of a work using different philosophies, or schools of thought. Critical theory can be used to understand all types of cultural productions.

There are many different critical theories. If you are analyzing literature, each theory asks you to look at the work from a different perspective. Some theories address social issues, while others focus on the writer's life or the time period in which the book was written or set. For example, the critical theory that asks how an author's life affected the work is called biographical criticism. Other common schools of criticism include historical criticism, feminist criticism, psychological criticism, and New Criticism, which examines a work solely within the context of the work itself.

What Is the Purpose of Critical Theory?

Critical theory can open your mind to new ways of thinking. It can help you evaluate a book from a new perspective, directing your attention to issues and messages you may not otherwise recognize in a work. For example, applying feminist criticism to a book may make you aware of female stereotypes perpetuated in the work. Applying a critical theory to a book helps you learn about the person who created it or the society that enjoyed it. You can also explore how the work is perceived by current cultures.

How Do You Apply Critical Theory?

You conduct a critique when you use a critical theory to examine and question a work. The theory you choose is a lens through which you can view the work, or a springboard for asking questions about the work. Applying a critical theory helps you think critically about the work. You are free to question the work and make an assertion about it. If you choose to examine a book using biographical theory, for example, you want to know how the author's personal background or education inspired or shaped the work. You could explore why the author was drawn to the story. For instance, are there any parallels between a particular character's life and the author's life?

Forming a Thesis

Ask your question and find answers in the work or other related materials. Then you can create a thesis. The thesis is the key point in your critique. It is your argument about the work based on the tenets, or beliefs, of the theory you are using. For example, if you are using biographical theory to ask how the author's life inspired the work, your thesis could be worded as follows: Writer Teng Xiong, raised in refugee camps in

> ### How to Make a Thesis Statement
>
> In a critique, a thesis statement typically appears at the end of the introductory paragraph. It is usually only one sentence long and states the author's main idea.

Southeast Asia, drew upon her experiences to write the novel *No Home for Me*.

Providing Evidence

Once you have formed a thesis, you must provide evidence to support it. Evidence might take the form of examples and quotations from the work itself—such as dialogue from a character. Articles about the book or personal interviews with the author might also support your ideas. You may wish to address what other critics have written about the work. Quotes from these individuals may help support your claim. If you find any quotes or examples that contradict your thesis, you will need to create an argument against them. For instance: Many critics have pointed to the protagonist of *No Home for Me* as a powerless victim of circumstances. However, in the chapter "My Destiny," she is clearly depicted as someone who seeks to shape her own future.

How to Support a Thesis Statement

A critique should include several arguments. Arguments support a thesis claim. An argument is one or two sentences long and is supported by evidence from the work being discussed.

Organize the arguments into paragraphs. These paragraphs make up the body of the critique.

In This Book

In this book, you will read summaries of famous works by writer Virginia Woolf, each followed by a critique. Each critique will use one theory and apply it to one work. Critical thinking sections will give you a chance to consider other theses and questions about the work. Did you agree with the author's application of the theory? What other questions are raised by the thesis and its arguments? You can also find out what other critics think about each particular book. Then, in the You Critique It section in the final pages of this book, you will have an opportunity to create your own critique.

Look for the Guides

Throughout the chapters that analyze the works, thesis statements have been highlighted. The box next to the thesis helps explain what questions are being raised about the work. Supporting arguments have been underlined. The boxes next to the arguments help explain how these points support the thesis. Look for these guides throughout each critique.

Author Virginia Woolf is one of the most well-known writers of the twentieth century.

2

A Closer Look at Virginia Woolf

Early Life

Virginia Woolf was born Adeline Virginia Stephen on January 25, 1882, into a prestigious upper-middle-class family in London, England. Her father, Leslie Stephen, was a well-known critic and held honorary doctorates from several universities, including Oxford and Cambridge in England. Virginia's mother, Julia Duckworth Stephen, exemplified the model Victorian woman; she was beautiful, well mannered, and self-sacrificing. Virginia had an older sister, Vanessa; an older brother, Thoby; and a younger brother, Adrian. She also had four half siblings from her parents' previous marriages.

As a child, Virginia had free rein of her father's library. She loved reading and began writing stories at a young age. Virginia received her education at home because her father did not believe women should go to school. Although she lacked a formal education, Virginia grew up in a literary household, and her parents encouraged her to read and write.

From Kensington to Bloomsbury

In 1895, when Virginia was 13 years old, Julia died after becoming ill with influenza, and Virginia experienced her first nervous breakdowns. She would continue to have nervous breakdowns throughout her lifetime. She suffered from symptoms similar to bipolar disorder. She also experienced hallucinations.

After their father died from cancer in 1904, Virginia and her siblings sold the Stephen family home. They moved from the fashionable Kensington neighborhood of London to Bloomsbury, a less fancy part of the city. In 1905, Virginia began teaching at Morley College in London. Bloomsbury was a popular spot for artists and intellectuals at that time. In Bloomsbury, Virginia became acquainted with important artists and writers such as Clive Bell, Lytton Strachey, and Leonard Woolf, known collectively as the

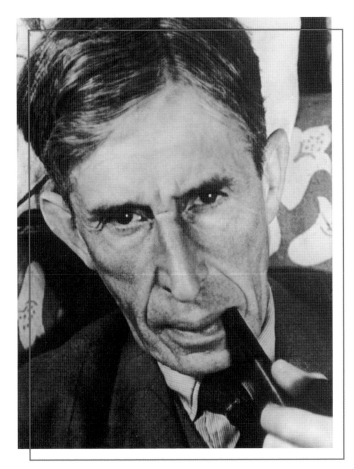

Leonard Woolf married Virginia in 1912. He helped her manage her depression throughout her life.

Bloomsbury Group, which started meeting in approximately 1907.

Virginia married Leonard Woolf in 1912. Leonard became as much Virginia's caretaker as her husband. He documented all of her nervous breakdowns and played a major role in her treatment. In 1917, the couple founded the Hogarth

Press. They published the works of famous authors such as E. M. Forster and T. S. Eliot.

Fame and Literary Recognition

Woolf had begun writing professionally in 1904, when she published a piece in the newspaper the *Guardian*. Shortly after her marriage to Leonard, she began working on her first novel. Her half brother Gerald Duckworth owned a publishing house and published her novel *The Voyage Out* in 1915.

Woolf was writing in the era of modernism, a European movement of the early twentieth century in which artists broke from traditional forms of art. She started writing more experimental fiction with her novel *Jacob's Room*, published in 1922. In *Jacob's Room*, Woolf experimented with modernist techniques such as fragmented writing, interior monologue, and multiple protagonists. *Jacob's Room* was not popular with critics, but the novel's publication put Woolf into contact with an important literary circle that included writers Vita Sackville-West and H. G. Wells. Sackville-West was the wife of author Harold Nicolson. Woolf and Sackville-West became friends and, in 1925, began

Author Vita Sackville-West became Woolf's lover for a short time, as well as the inspiration for *Orlando*.

a brief but passionate romantic relationship. Their strong friendship remained even after the romantic relationship ended.

Woolf continued putting out works in the 1920s. She published *Mrs. Dalloway* in 1925 and *To the Lighthouse* in 1927. In 1928, she published *Orlando*, a novel inspired by the family history of Sackville-West. The novel pokes fun at academic historical writing and a number of literary texts. The book earned Woolf public recognition for her writing. The publication of *Orlando* also led to more fame and speaking engagements for Woolf.

In October 1928, she was asked to lecture at Newnham and Girton, two women's colleges in the Cambridge system. Her lecture notes from these speaking engagements produced her famous essay *A Room of One's Own*, published in 1929. This essay became one of the most famous feminist texts of all time.

Last Days

Toward the end of her life, Woolf became increasingly depressed about the state of the world. London was severely bombed in the early days of World War II (1939–1945). Woolf moved to the British countryside after her house was damaged by bombs in 1940 but complained that she missed London terribly. In her journals from this time period she wrote often of her love of London.

As the war progressed, Woolf and her husband started discussing the consequences of a German invasion and the possibility of writers such as themselves being imprisoned. As news of the war became more serious, Woolf's mood darkened. During the early period of World War II, Woolf's nervous attacks flared up again. She became increasingly fearful that she was going insane. On the morning of March 28, 1941, Woolf slipped

After suffering from nervous breakdowns for more than 45 years, Woolf took her own life in 1941.

through her garden quietly without her husband noticing. She continued down to the River Ouse, put a large rock in her pocket, walked out into the water, and drowned herself. In her suicide note to Leonard, she wrote that she was on the verge of another nervous breakdown and could not put either of them through the pain of another episode.

During her lifetime Woolf wrote nine novels, one play, more than five volumes of essays, portraits, memoirs, and reviews, more than 11 volumes of diaries and letters, and 46 short stories. She is still considered one of the great minds of the twentieth century, and her work continues to impact feminism and literature today.

In the 2002 film *The Hours*, actress Nicole Kidman played Woolf as she was writing *Mrs. Dalloway*.

Chapter

3

An Overview of
Mrs. Dalloway

Mrs. Dalloway takes place five years after the end of World War I (1914–1918). The story occurs over the course of one June day in London in 1923. The narrative travels backward and forward in time and frequently jumps from one character's perspective to another's. As the novel begins, Clarissa Dalloway, a woman in her early fifties, is considering the preparations she must make for a party she is giving later that evening. While running errands, she encounters Hugh Whitbread, a friend from her youth. She remembers her old friends Sally Seton and Peter Walsh. Both were quite rebellious and eccentric as youths.

Clarissa thinks about Peter, with whom she had been in love and who had once proposed to her, though she rejected him. They had argued and criticized each other frequently. While Peter hated British social traditions and the snobbery of the rich, Clarissa found comfort in these customs and married a traditional, wealthy man, Richard Dalloway. Clarissa has embraced her upper-class life. She looks down upon marriages between people of different social classes, referring to a woman who married above her class as a "cockatoo."[1] However, Clarissa admired Peter for his intellect and his unique way of seeing the world. Peter loved Clarissa's enthusiasm for life and her capacity for emotion.

A Figure of the Past

Not long after Clarissa returns home from her errands, Peter unexpectedly visits her. He has just returned to Great Britain after living in India for several years. His marriage has failed and his career is not a success. He is engaged to a married woman, Daisy, in India. Peter has returned to London to arrange a divorce for Daisy. As he tells Clarissa about his relationship with Daisy, he begins crying.

He and Clarissa reminisce about the past, but the past brings back painful memories for Peter. He still resents Clarissa for refusing his marriage proposal.

Just then, Clarissa's daughter, Elizabeth, returns home. Peter quickly leaves the house. Walking around London, he thinks about his life, the differences between London and India, and about Clarissa. Peter falls asleep and dreams of a solitary traveler. When he awakes, he recalls when Clarissa shunned a woman who had a child out of wedlock. He thinks about when Clarissa and Richard first met and how he had predicted they would marry.

The Present

While Clarissa is running errands, Richard and Hugh eat lunch. On the way home, Richard admires a memorial to Queen Victoria and thinks of his wife, Clarissa. He buys her flowers and decides he will tell her he loves her. When he sees her, however, he cannot say the words, but she understands what he wants to say.

Meanwhile, Elizabeth is upstairs with her friend Miss Kilman. Miss Kilman is very religious and complains often. Clarissa does not like Miss Kilman because she is unattractive and poor. Clarissa feels Miss Kilman purposely makes people feel guilty for having money.

A Broken Soldier

Earlier in the day, former soldier Septimus
Warren Smith and his Italian wife, Lucrezia, sit
in the park. Septimus suffers from shell shock, a
psychological disorder common in many World
War I veterans. Septimus's doctor, Dr. Holmes,
has told Lucrezia that Septimus needs distractions.
Everywhere he goes, Septimus thinks he sees his
friend Evans, who was killed in World War I.

Septimus is lost in his own thoughts. He
stares off into space and talks to himself. This
frightens and worries Lucrezia. The couple has an
appointment to see the well-known specialist Sir
William Bradshaw about Septimus's condition.
Septimus hates doctors but agrees to go. At the
appointment, Bradshaw tells Lucrezia that Septimus
has suicidal tendencies and must be treated at a
home for the mentally disturbed.

Septimus and Lucrezia spend a happy evening
together in their home. Lucrezia makes a hat for
their neighbor, and Septimus helps her arrange
it. He feels satisfied when he sees the finished
hat. Dr. Holmes arrives to check in on Septimus.
Lucrezia runs down the stairs to tell him to go
away; Septimus is doing well and she does not

want the doctor's visit to ruin his mood. Dr. Holmes forces his way into Septimus and Lucrezia's home. Septimus, not wanting to face any more doctors, jumps out the window and commits suicide.

The Party

That evening, Clarissa's party begins, and Clarissa worries it will be a failure. Clarissa is quite flattered when the prime minister arrives, and people remark on how ordinary he looks.

Sir Bradshaw and Lady Bradshaw arrive and discuss Septimus's death. At first Clarissa is upset that they bring up death at her party, but then she thinks more about Septimus. She somehow feels responsible for his death, but then she decides Septimus is courageous for killing himself. She thinks that if she were to kill herself, it would be only to find greater happiness.

Peter and Sally arrive, but Clarissa cannot speak to them for long since she has to attend to other guests. Sally and Peter talk about the past and find that neither of them has changed much. Peter wonders where Clarissa is. Sally gets up to speak to Richard. Peter sees Clarissa arriving to speak to him and is filled with both terror and excitement.

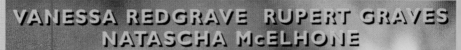

VANESSA REDGRAVE RUPERT GRAVES
NATASCHA McELHONE

FROM THE DIRECTOR OF THE
ACADEMY AWARD-WINNING
ANTONIA'S LINE

MRS DALLOWAY

"AN IMPECCABLE PIECE OF CINEMA"

Both the novel and the 1997 film adaption of *Mrs. Dalloway* reflect the cultural and social trends following World War I.

4

How to Apply Historical Criticism to *Mrs. Dalloway*

What Is Historical Criticism?

Historical criticism focuses on the historical background in which a piece of literature was written. It looks at what was happening in the culture at the time. A historical critic must be able to identify the cultural and historical influences of a character's actions and understand any reference to specific cultural or historical events mentioned in the text.

Applying Historical Criticism to *Mrs. Dalloway*

World War I shook Great Britain's sense of unity as well as its belief in itself as a world power. The unprecedented amount of violence as well as the collapse of social barriers during the war profoundly changed British culture. Men of all social classes fought side by side against the Germans. Bombs were dropped on London for the first time. Millions of soldiers came home traumatized by war. As a result, many British citizens began questioning British traditions, including its rigid class system and monarchy. The characters in *Mrs. Dalloway* represent the results of these cultural shifts on British society. The characters' questioning and defending of pre–World War I customs and the English class system as well as their psychological trauma display the effects of World War I on British society.

Septimus's struggle with shell shock and society's inability to deal with his needs reflects the struggle of World War I soldiers as they returned home. Shell shock was a trauma common in soldiers who survived the war. Shell shock is today known as post-traumatic stress disorder (PTSD). More than 80,000

Thesis Statement

The thesis statement sets up the author's critique. This thesis statement reads: "The characters' questioning and defending of pre–World War I customs and the English class system as well as their psychological trauma display the effects of World War I on British society." The author focuses the essay on how a real historical incident, World War I, is reflected in *Mrs. Dalloway*.

Argument One

The first argument reads: "Septimus's struggle with shell shock and society's inability to deal with his needs reflects the struggle of World War I soldiers as they returned home." The author focuses on the character Septimus and the way he reflects the plight of real World War I veterans.

soldiers were discharged from the British army during World War I due to shell shock. People suffering from PTSD often feel emotionally numb at first. They have no response to what happened to them. Like Septimus, many soldiers who survived World War I felt guilty for having survived when so many others died. They suffered nightmares and flashbacks from the war. Sudden noises triggered memories of the traumatic incident. In *Mrs. Dalloway*, Septimus jumps at the noise of a motorcar backfiring. He has conversations with his

Even after returning home, many World War I soldiers never fully recovered from their experiences in the war.

friend Evans who was killed in the war. He is no longer the man he once was. His wife, Lucrezia, thinks of him: "it was cowardly for a man to say he would kill himself; but Septimus had fought; he was brave; he was not Septimus now."[1] Eventually, Septimus commits suicide, jumping out of a window rather than face the doctor attempting to treat him. When he does so, Dr. Holmes calls him a "coward," indicating he did not understand the depths of Septimus's inner turmoil and therefore would have been incapable of effectively treating him.[2] Dr. Holmes's response shows British society's failure to correctly attend to these suffering veterans. Shell shock left many young men incapacitated. Some never recovered and were unable to support their families or live normal, healthy lives.

Mrs. Dalloway makes references to certain social norms that were prevalent during a time in British history known as the Edwardian era. The contrast between Clarissa and Richard Dalloway's appreciation for the Edwardian traditions of the past

---

Argument Two

The second argument states: "The contrast between Clarissa and Richard Dalloway's appreciation for the Edwardian traditions of the past and Peter's disgust for them exemplifies a Great Britain stuck between its past and present." The author chooses two main points of view from the book to illustrate the mood in Great Britain after World War I.

and Peter's disgust for them exemplifies a Great Britain stuck between its past and present. The Edwardian era lasted from 1901 to 1910, when Edward VII was the king of Great Britain. During this time, great social change occurred throughout the country. Though the British upper-class lifestyle was still sought after and powerful, it became less exclusive and was not necessarily limited to people who were born into the aristocracy.

Clarissa is a symbol of upper-class British life and upholds traditional Edwardian ideas of social propriety. She married a conventional, upper-class man and had a daughter. She loves the rituals of planning parties, such as finding the perfect flowers. Her opinions about social propriety are bound by class stereotypes. In many ways, she proves herself to be the snob that Peter accuses her of being. She is outraged when she learns that a woman of her acquaintance had a child out of wedlock, vowing never to speak to the woman again. Clarissa's outrage reflects Edwardian values of chastity in women. At her party, she pays more attention to people she considers more socially significant, instead of speaking to her old friends Peter and Sally, showing her elitist Edwardian way of thinking. Like his wife, Richard also has an attachment to the comfort of traditions. When he thinks back to when he saw Queen Victoria in London, he thinks how much he "liked continuity; and the sense of the handing on of traditions of the past."[3]

Peter, on the other hand, utterly rejects British conventions. The solitary traveler in his dream vows to "never go back to the lamplight, to the sitting room," which is a snub to British social customs.[4] In contrast to Edwardian ideals of family life, Peter seems to have no family at all. He is engaged to a woman already the wife of a major in the Indian army. At this time, India was under British control. Peter's choice of a woman whose husband represents the British government and Peter's utter disregard for their marriage can be further seen as a rejection of British tradition. His unconventional relationships defy the Edwardian emphasis on the importance of marriage.

Many British citizens at the time felt disillusioned by the war and had lost faith in the old way of doing things. However, this disillusionment went beyond British customs and conventions. The characters in *Mrs. Dalloway* show much of British society's disenchantment with the hierarchical class system of old. In many ways, World War I shook British society's traditions to the core. Up until this time an extremely rigid class system existed in Great Britain in which people from different social classes barely interacted with one another. But World War I changed this. For the first time, men from all classes fought side by side to defend their country. Women worked together to keep the country running while the men were at war. Clarissa's changing behavior toward social classes is symbolic of these class shifts. In the beginning of the novel, Clarissa is judgmental of the lower class, believing the upper and lower classes should be kept separate. As a young woman, she once described a woman who married above her class as a "cockatoo," indicating that she was dressing and acting above her station.[5] However, times have changed. Elizabeth, Clarissa's daughter, befriends Miss Kilman, who is poor and working class. Clarissa is forced to welcome the woman into

Argument Three

The author's third argument states: "The characters in *Mrs. Dalloway* show much of British society's disenchantment with the hierarchical class system of old." The author gives a final example of the characters' disillusionment, this time focusing on the social shifts taking place in the class system.

her home even though she disapproves of her. This shows that time has passed and ideas of strict class divisions are changing in Great Britain. Clarissa must adapt. These changes in class indicate that social conventions are breaking down and the strict class system of old is weakening.

Septimus's psychological trauma, Peter's and the Dalloways' contrasting belief systems, and the examples of Great Britain's changing class system are all indicative of the changes in British culture as a result of World War I. Septimus's symptoms of shell shock represent a generation of psychologically disturbed former soldiers. Peter's attack on British tradition as well as Richard and Clarissa's defense of it symbolize two prominent but opposing views at the time. While some British citizens were disillusioned and no longer respected British tradition, others clung to it for security. However, none remained completely unaffected by the events of World War I.

Conclusion
The conclusion partially restates the thesis and summarizes the supporting arguments. This conclusion leaves the reader with a new thought: that no British citizen was unaffected by World War I.

Thinking Critically

Now it is your turn to assess the critique. Consider these questions:

1. The author's thesis statement asserts the effect of World War I on British society can be seen in the characters of *Mrs. Dalloway*. Do you think the arguments effectively support this thesis? Why or why not?

2. The author compares and contrasts the Dalloways' and Peter's views on British conventions. What do the other characters' views on these traditions suggest?

3. The author's conclusion suggests no British citizens were unaffected by World War I. Do you see other examples of World War I's effect on British culture in *Mrs. Dalloway*?

Other Approaches

The previous essay was only one example of a historical critique of *Mrs. Dalloway*. Another essay might more closely consider the various historical transitions Great Britain was going through in 1923. India, a former British colony, was in the middle of its independence movement. Many British citizens had rejected the rigid Edwardian value system of old. The mass death of more than 12 million people in World War I struck the British with a sense of fear and isolation. Another essay might consider the references to death and loneliness made by Clarissa Dalloway and Septimus and the way these allusions reflect attitudes of British society at that time.

British Imperialism

Up until the 1920s, Britain had been one of the most powerful countries in the world and held much territory abroad. One of these territories was India. Many British men, similar to Peter Walsh, went to work for the British government in India. However, in the 1920s, India was in the midst of its struggle for independence from Great Britain. In *Mrs. Dalloway* there are numerous references to India as well as South Africa, both British colonies.

A possible thesis for an essay studying British imperialism could be: Peter's reflections on India mirror British imperialist attitudes toward India. One argument in this critique could make parallels between Peter's references to India being uncivilized and British imperialist goals to civilize India by building railroads and trying to convert Indians to Christianity.

Thoughts of Death

Many British citizens were affected by the brutality of the war as well as the impact of mass death upon society. Death was everywhere and along with it came feelings of isolation and fear of death. In *Mrs. Dalloway*, many of the characters are preoccupied with thoughts of death as well as with their own loneliness.

A possible thesis statement for this idea could be: The characters' doubts, psychological deterioration, and loneliness reflect a British society profoundly affected by death. Potential arguments to support this thesis could include a closer look at Septimus's thoughts of suicide and his fixation on his deceased friend, Evans.

Woolf's essay *A Room of One's Own* is one of her most famous feminist works.

5

An Overview of
A Room of One's Own

Woolf originally wrote her famous essay *A Room of One's Own* from speeches she gave at two women's colleges on the subject of women and fiction. Woolf's thesis is: "A woman must have money and a room of her own if she is to write fiction."[1] Instead of writing from her own perspective, Woolf uses a fictional female narrator to address the subject. The narrator makes many references to her aunt, who left her an inheritance upon her death. The narrator claims that without this inheritance she would not have been able to become a writer.

An Unaccompanied Woman

The narrator begins with a visit to a men's college that is part of Oxbridge, a fusion of Oxford and Cambridge Universities. She tries to think about the issue of women and fiction but is interrupted by a school guard who wants her to get off the grass because only men are allowed on the grass. She quickly leaves the grass and returns to her thoughts about women and fiction. The narrator goes to the library to look up a particular essay she thinks might help her. Once there, she is told that women cannot enter the library without being accompanied by a man who is an academic member of the university. Leaning against a wall, she observes the students and professors, noting the university looks like "a sanctuary in which are preserved rare types which would soon be obsolete."[2] Later, at the women's college Fernham, the narrator describes how poor a meal is there compared to a luncheon at Oxbridge. She notes how much nicer the men's college is than the women's college.

The scene changes to London. The narrator is still thinking about women and fiction, but now she is at the library at the British Museum. At this library, she finds many essays written about women, but men have written all of them. Most of the essays refer to women as the inferior gender and claim women are incapable of logical thought. However, the narrator notes fictional depictions of women

are quite the opposite. Women are portrayed as saintly, clever, fierce, and strong. She wonders at this discrepancy. She asserts that the main reason men try to keep women inferior is to make sure men remain superior in society.

The narrator is quickly ushered off the lawn at Oxbridge because only men are allowed on the grass.

At home, the narrator is disappointed by how little truth her research at the British Museum uncovered. She considers the importance of literature during the sixteenth century, when William Shakespeare was writing his plays and sonnets. The narrator comes to the conclusion that a woman in Shakespeare's day could not have possibly been a successful writer due to the constraints of society. To support this idea, the narrator envisions Judith Shakespeare, an imaginary sister of William Shakespeare. Judith is as gifted as her brother but is unable to realize her talent because of the pressures of her family and society to conform to a traditional female role. Prevented from pursuing her gift, Judith's life falls into ruin and, the narrator imagines, she commits suicide.

The Feminine Literary Voice

After considering the impossibility of a woman becoming a successful writer during Shakespeare's time, the narrator goes on to give the reader a short summary of women writers in history. She makes references to famous nineteenth-century female authors, including Anne, Emily, and Charlotte Brontë and Jane Austen. She notes that all these women wrote novels, which the narrator believes is the result of writing in a shared space, such as a sitting room, and a lack of formal education. These factors made the novel format most accessible for Austen and the Brontës. She points out that these women all had the same style of writing, focusing on social issues instead of themes of war. It is here that she identifies a feminine literary voice. The narrator argues that both male and female narrative voices need to be represented in literature.

The narrator then discusses "books by the living."[3] She considers the fictional twentieth-century author Mary Carmichael, influenced by female authors from the past, but whom the narrator believes is not as talented as Austen. Still, through Carmichael's depiction of a friendship between two women, the narrator recognizes that Carmichael has written a book that considers the relationships of women with women, rather than the relationships of women with men. The narrator concludes that in 100 years and with money and her own space to write, Carmichael could become a poet.

The next morning, the narrator wakes up to the conclusion that writers should not consider their own sex when writing. Woolf herself then takes over the essay's narration from her own point of view. She acknowledges the close relationship between material goods and an author's freedom to write. She emphasizes the importance of making money for women, not only to support themselves but also to begin a female literary tradition that can gain public recognition and historical significance.

Woolf, shown with famous writer T. S. Eliot, believed women were
at a distinct disadvantage to men in the world of literature.

6

How to Apply Feminist Criticism to *A Room of One's Own*

No.2

What Is Feminist Criticism?

Feminist literary criticism refers to the study of literature written by women or the analysis of a text with a focus on female characters or gender roles. Feminist criticism challenges stereotypes of or traditional ideas about women. It maintains that Western civilization is predominantly patriarchal. Feminist criticism assumes that the values of a patriarchal society are reflected in literature. A major debate among feminists is whether women writers should establish a distinctly feminine style of writing in contrast to that of men. Some argue that because men have dominated literature for so long, it is important they be countered by a female literary voice. Others believe there is no difference between the ways men and women think, but rather there is a difference between how men and women are valued.

Applying Feminist Criticism to *A Room of One's Own*

In *A Room of One's Own*, Woolf's main argument is that in order for women to succeed as writers they must have money and a room of their own to work in. In Woolf's eyes, women can only succeed as writers when they have the same resources available to them that men do. *A Room of One's Own* argues that men have historically been more successful than women due to their access to education, money, and personal autonomy.

Throughout the essay, external patriarchal forces interrupt the narrator's train of thought. While walking, the narrator is instructed to stay off the grass because only men have access to the university's lawns. Though the narrator moves to the

---

Thesis Statement

The thesis statement reads: "*A Room of One's Own* argues that men have historically been more successful than women due to their access to education, money, and personal autonomy." The author spends the rest of the essay discussing how a lack of these factors has impacted women's success in literature.

Argument One

The author sets up the essay with the first argument: "Throughout the essay, external patriarchal forces interrupt the narrator's train of thought." The author starts by discussing how the narrator is directly affected by a patriarchal society.

path, she has lost her train of thought on women and fiction. Later, the narrator is physically barred from educating herself when she is told she cannot enter the university library without being accompanied by a man. These interruptions exemplify how women historically have been restricted from education. They also symbolize the interruptions women suffer that impede them from being free to write. Women are given less personal freedom than men and, therefore, are not allowed access to resources that are necessary for writing, such as libraries.

When Woolf's narrator researches the subject of women at the British Museum, she is surprised to find all the articles about women are written by men. The narrator realizes male perspectives dictate the way women are represented in education about women's literature. Because men historically have had authority over what is published, they were able to decide what was written about women. Men's authority over literature allows them to shape society's perceptions of

> **Argument Two**
>
> The author takes the previous argument a step further with the second argument: "The narrator realizes male perspectives dictate the way women are represented in education about women's literature." This argument focuses on how male perspectives control representations of female writers.

women. This supports the feminist view that men dictate women's behavior. The overwhelming male presence in literature exposes the patriarchy of education. It reveals that, contrary to popular belief, literature is not objective but is biased by the male perspective. Furthermore, many of these articles refer to women as mentally inferior to men. One maintains that women "have no character at all."[1] By pointing out these descriptions the narrator emphasizes recurrent negative depictions of women in literature. By highlighting these stereotypes' frequent occurrence, the narrator exposes the history of female subordination in literature.

The narrator depicts writing as a profession that women historically have been barred from entering into. The narrator uses the example of Judith Shakespeare, William Shakespeare's fictional sister, to exemplify this point. Woolf points out that even if Judith were as good a writer as William, she would not have been permitted to write. She would have had no formal education, and her

Argument Three

The third argument states: "The narrator depicts writing as a profession that women historically have been barred from entering into." The author focuses on the narrator's discussion of Judith Shakespeare to support the argument.

The narrator asserts that if playwright Shakespeare had an equally talented sister, she would not have been able to become a successful writer.

parents would have instructed her to get married and have a family instead of write. If she chose to write anyway, she would have had little spare time and would have had to do so secretly. In Woolf's story, Judith ends up committing suicide due to her inability to pursue her creative goals.

In a description of women's poetry, the narrator discusses a female poet writing about the trials of domestic life. This example shows that women have a different set of responsibilities that deter them from writing. They are expected to take care of the household and children. They are not allowed the free time required for writing literature. The narrator believes there is a universal assumption that men have superior intellects to women. Because of this assumption, men are granted the free time for thought and creativity while women are not.

<u>Woolf defines success in materialistic terms, an area in which men have an advantage.</u> Her description of the men's college is majestic in comparison to that of Fernham, the women's college. She describes how meager the dinner at Fernham is and, in contrast, describes the majesty of Oxbridge's campus.

Woolf barely mentions the intellectual merits of either college, but rather defines the success of each school based on material terms. In these terms, she shows that Oxbridge has more wealth than Fernham. This symbolizes the difference in wealth between men and women in general at this time.

Woolf's narrator frequently speaks of the good fortune she had in having an aunt who left her a large sum of money upon her death. She infers that she would not have been a writer without this monetary gift. Woolf feels that money is necessary for the success of any literary career. She maintains that to write, one must be in a position to live comfortably. She believes money buys writers the freedom to live comfortably and devote their time to their craft. Woolf urges women to make a living in order to break down social barriers so women can be afforded the same opportunities as men. She writes, "Money dignifies what is frivolous if unpaid for," meaning nothing has value in the eyes of society unless it is given a price.[2] Woolf implores women to prove their work is worth something by giving it monetary value. She depicts money as the great equalizer between the sexes. She implies that if women were given money for their writing, they would eventually achieve the same social status as men.

A Room of One's Own argues that men's literary success over women is based on men's access to education, money, and personal autonomy. Women, on the other hand, have been denied access to higher education, have been forced to be financially

Conclusion
The conclusion partially restates the thesis, now supported by the arguments. It offers Woolf's ideas to increase equality between men and women.

dependent on men, and have been misrepresented and underestimated. Woolf encourages women to start earning money for themselves so that they might break down social barriers. She believes this financial freedom will put women on the path to equality with men.

Thinking Critically

Now it is your turn to assess the critique.
Consider these questions:

1. The author's thesis asserts that men have been more successful than women because they have better access to freedom, education, and other factors. Do the author's arguments support the thesis? Why or why not?

2. What is the author's strongest argument? What is the weakest? What other evidence from the text could be used to support the thesis?

3. A conclusion should summarize the supporting arguments and partially restate the thesis. Does this conclusion do a good job summing up the essay? How could it be improved?

Other Approaches

There are many different ways to approach a work from a feminist perspective. An alternate essay could argue that Woolf makes clear distinctions between men's and women's subject matter in literature as well as in their educations. Yet another critique might argue that Woolf concludes both men and women are capable of writing from male and female perspectives. This conclusion infers that neither men nor women naturally write in a certain way, but instead, each adopts a certain writing style stereotypical of their gender.

Female Literature

Throughout *A Room of One's Own*, Woolf makes distinctions between male and female writing. One way to write an essay from this perspective is to analyze the ways in which Woolf portrays these differences. She maintains that while men write about war and justice, women write about human emotion and behavior. She argues that literature is biased in men's favor and lacks a truly objective perspective because it does not include women's voices.

A thesis for this idea might read: Throughout *A Room of One's Own*, Woolf makes distinctions between male and female writing, illustrating that both voices are necessary to fully depict the human experience.

The Sameness of Gender

In *A Room of One's Own* Woolf points out the differences between men's schools and women's schools. But because she focuses on physical features rather than academic accomplishments, she seems to say that men's academic advantage over women is purely materialistic. Furthermore, she cites women's writing throughout history to show that women can write just as well as men.

A thesis statement for an argument considering these ideas might read: Woolf argues that both men and women are capable of writing from either gender's perspective, implying there is no difference between the way men and women write.

Woolf, shown with her brother-in-law, spent many summers at a beach house similar to the one owned by the Ramsays in *To the Lighthouse*.

An Overview of
To The Lighthouse

To The Lighthouse follows a Victorian family,
the Ramsays. The Ramsays have eight children:
Jasper, Roger, Prue, Rose, Nancy, Cam, Andrew,
and James. The novel takes place in the family's
summer home in Hebrides, Scotland. The narrative
is disjointed and switches back and forth in time
and from one character's point of view to another's.
There is very little action or dialogue in the
novel; instead it focuses on a series of details and
observations made by each character. The novel is
split into three sections that take place several years
apart from each other.

The Window

This first part of the novel takes place over
the course of one day while the Ramsays are

vacationing at their summer home with several guests. Staying with the Ramsays are Augustus Carmichael, a reclusive poet; Charles Tansley, a young philosopher; Lily Briscoe, an artist and unmarried woman; William Bankes, an old friend of the Ramsays; and Minta Doyle and Paul Rayley, young friends of the Ramsays.

The novel begins with James, the Ramsay's youngest son, expressing a desire to go see the nearby lighthouse. Mr. Ramsay dashes James's hopes by saying the weather will not permit such a venture. To protect James's feelings, Mrs. Ramsay says the weather still might turn out to be fine. James strongly loves his mother and passionately hates his father. Later that evening, Mr. Tansley tells Mrs. Ramsay the weather is poor and they will certainly not be able to go to the lighthouse the next day. Mrs. Ramsay tries comforting James by telling him the weather may improve in the morning.

Minta, Paul, Nancy, and Andrew go for a walk before dinner. Mrs. Ramsay has encouraged Paul to propose to Minta, and he does so on this walk. Meanwhile, Mrs. Ramsay enjoys some precious solitude in the garden. Mr. Ramsay observes her and thinks she looks miserable. He wants to protect her but does not want to disturb her. He knows he plays a big part in her worries. Mr. Ramsay is emotionally dependent on Mrs. Ramsay. He constantly seeks her approval. He is insecure about his work as a writer and philosopher and fears he will die without being acknowledged for his achievements. He often acts like a child. However, Mrs. Ramsay reveres him and indulges his childlike behavior.

Lily and Bankes engage in conversation while Lily paints in the garden. They speak about art, and Lily feels as if they have shared something very intimate. She admires Bankes, and it is obvious the two of them mutually respect each other. Mrs. Ramsay sees them interacting and thinks they should marry. Lily assumes this is what Mrs. Ramsay is thinking and vows she will not marry Bankes.

The family and their guests sit down to a special dinner Mrs. Ramsay has planned. Mr. Ramsay is visibly annoyed when Carmichael asks for another bowl of soup after Mr. Ramsay has stopped eating. However, with one look, Mrs. Ramsay is able to ease Mr. Ramsay's foul mood. Nobody is speaking to Mr. Tansley; with her eyes, Mrs. Ramsay implores Lily to speak to him. Lily dislikes Mr. Tansley because he has told her women cannot paint.

However, she tries to engage him in conversation. The interaction is forced and insincere. Lily reflects on how she cannot act as women are supposed to act. She thinks about her art and how important it is to her. Paul sits next to Mrs. Ramsay. She can tell he has proposed to Minta and feels a twinge of jealousy. As the dinner ends, Mrs. Ramsay reflects on how the moment and the joy she and her guests shared are already part of the past.

After dinner, Mrs. Ramsay goes upstairs to check on her young children. James once again asks if they can go to the lighthouse in the morning. This time, Mrs. Ramsay tells him no but feels guilty for disappointing him.

She returns downstairs to sit with Mr. Ramsay in the sitting room. Mr. Ramsay thinks his wife looks more beautiful than ever. He wants her to tell him that she loves him. Mrs. Ramsay sees this, and though she does love him, she is incapable of expressing it. Instead she tells him he was correct, and they will not be able to go to the lighthouse in the morning. Mr. Ramsay understands she means she loves him.

Time Passes

This part of the novel moves much more quickly and takes place over the course of several years. Mrs. Ramsay dies suddenly, and Mr. Ramsay is distraught. The old Ramsay house begins deteriorating. Prue, the Ramsay's eldest daughter, marries but then dies in childbirth. World War I begins and ends. Andrew, one of the Ramsay's older children, is killed in the fighting. The summer home continues decaying. Then, ten years after the novel began, Lily returns to the Ramsay summer home.

The Lighthouse

Carmichael and the surviving Ramsay family have also returned to the summer home. Mr. Ramsay insists that he, his daughter Cam, and James go to the lighthouse the next morning. However, Mr. Ramsay gets upset when they get a late start. He goes to Lily seeking sympathy, but this makes her uncomfortable. All she can do is tell him she likes his boots, which makes him laugh.

Cam and James are grumpy and sullen, resentful of their father because they think he is tyrannical. Despite this, Mr. Ramsay, Cam, and James set off for the lighthouse. Lily stays in the garden.

In the garden, Lily decides she will finish the portrait of Mrs. Ramsay and James that she started many years ago. She thinks about Paul and Minta, and imagines that their marriage has failed. She thinks of Mrs. Ramsay and how she felt nothing upon her death. Now, however, she feels anger. Then, she starts missing Mrs. Ramsay terribly and calls out her name. She wishes Carmichael would speak to her but he is asleep. She looks out to sea for Mr. Ramsay's boat. She reflects on how the distance makes her fonder of him. She wishes to comfort him now.

Meanwhile, in the boat, James is brooding about his father while he steers and mans the sail. He has wanted his father's approval his entire life but has never gotten it. Cam is growing frustrated with her brother's attitude. She wishes he would forgive their father. Finally, they get to the lighthouse. Mr. Ramsay tells James he did a good job sailing the boat. Cam knows this is the validation James has been seeking for a long time. However, James's attitude toward his father does not appear to change.

On shore, Lily looks out to sea and knows the Ramsays must have landed at the lighthouse. Carmichael is now standing beside her and also

notes that the Ramsays must have reached the shore. Lily thinks that even though she and Carmichael have not spoken, they must be thinking the same thing. Lily puts the final touches on her painting, feeling a sense of relief that it is finally finished.

The Godrevy lighthouse near the Stephen family's summer home in Cornwall, England, was Woolf's inspiration for *To the Lighthouse.*

Many connections can be made between Woolf's personal life and her literary works.

How to Apply Biographical Criticism to *To the Lighthouse*

No. 2

What Is Biographical Criticism?

Biographical critics believe an author's life is connected to his or her work. They make comparisons between an author's literature and his or her life. Biographical critics believe knowing the author's background helps a reader interpret and understand the author's writing. These critics consider the race, gender, educational background, social status, and family influence of the author and how these factors may have affected the author's work. A biographical critic looks for ways a text provides clues about an author's personal life. The critic examines whether the text reflects the author's beliefs.

Applying Biographical Criticism to *To the Lighthouse*

Woolf often referred to her mother, Julia, as the model of Victorian womanhood. She was self-sacrificing yet firm in her values and beliefs. The character of Mrs. Ramsay is similar to Julia in many ways. The two women were both devoted to their families, very involved in their friends' and families' lives, and firm believers in Victorian ideals. The similarities between Mrs. Ramsay and Julia suggest Woolf based the character Mrs. Ramsay on her own mother.

Mrs. Ramsay has similar characteristics and mannerisms to Julia. Woolf described a strange sadness as one of her earliest childhood impressions of her mother. Leslie, Woolf's father, often described his wife as "melancholy" in his journals.[1] Many historians believe, as did Woolf herself, that Julia adopted this trait after the loss of her first husband. It was said

> **Thesis Statement**
>
> The thesis statement reads: "The similarities between Mrs. Ramsay and Julia suggest Woolf based the character Mrs. Ramsay on her own mother." The author spends the rest of the critique comparing Mrs. Ramsay to Julia.

> **Argument One**
>
> The first argument reads: "Mrs. Ramsay has similar characteristics and mannerisms to Julia." The author starts by comparing the two women's tendencies toward sadness.

Woolf saw her mother, Julia, as the model Victorian woman.

she often lay over the grave of her dead husband in grief. Julia once wrote to Leslie, "I have got so used to a shadow everywhere that I don't know if life is possible for me."[2]

Julia's characteristic sadness is mirrored in Mrs. Ramsay's acute awareness of death and change. All through the novel Mrs. Ramsay thinks of death and about how no happiness ever lasts.

After a pleasant dinner, Mrs. Ramsay becomes preoccupied by the idea that it is already in the past. She is often caught in these sad moments when she is alone, such as when Mr. Ramsay spies her sitting on the lawn thinking.

Julia and Mrs. Ramsay both have emotionally dependent husbands who often behave like children. Woolf describes Mr. Ramsay as self-obsessed and childlike in his need for attention. He throws a plate through a window when he finds an insect in his milk. He broods over what he considers to be the failure of his career. He frets over Carmichael asking for another bowl of soup. Woolf also describes how Mr. Ramsay tries to force people to give him sympathy. Yet he is easily appeased by Mrs. Ramsay, who in one look subdues Mr. Ramsay's anger about the soup. Woolf writes in regard to Mr. Ramsay, "There was nobody she [Mrs. Ramsay] reverenced as she reverenced him [Mr. Ramsay]."[3] Mrs. Ramsay restores his self-esteem by telling him Mr. Tansley greatly admires his work.

Argument Two

With the second argument, the author shifts the essay to discuss Julia's and Mrs. Ramsay's relationships with their husbands. The second argument reads: "Julia and Mrs. Ramsay both have emotionally dependent husbands who often behave like children."

Like Mr. Ramsay, Woolf's father often threw fits and was known to fly into rages over minor setbacks. Woolf and her siblings described their father's needs as like those of a child. Leslie was extremely emotionally dependent on Julia, constantly needing her to confirm he was a genius and his work was important, which she willingly did. He wrote her letters in which he admitted he sometimes complained only to get sympathy

Woolf viewed her father, Leslie, as a difficult and sometimes childlike man.

from her. When Julia was away nursing the sick, a common pastime for upper-class women of the Victorian era, Leslie wrote to her in anger, demanding she come back to take care of him and the children. Woolf and her siblings often speculated that their mother died from exhaustion due to the pressure of their father's demands.

<u>Still, both Mrs. Ramsay and Julia remained devoted to their husbands, despite the men's outrageous behaviors.</u> Julia revered her husband. She had read his writings and greatly admired his mind. Despite her husband's childlike behavior, Julia took special efforts to appease him. She sacrificed her solitude and free time for the well-being of her husband and family. She considered this self-sacrifice to be a female responsibility. Mrs. Ramsay also feels the need to sacrifice her own well-being to meet her husband's needs. She tolerates Mr. Ramsay's temper when he curses at her over something trivial. Mrs. Ramsay is sensitive to her husband's constant

---

Argument Three

Now that the author has established Mr. Ramsay's and Leslie's similarities, the author moves on to the third argument, which discusses Mrs. Ramsay's and Julia's devotion to their husbands. The third argument states: "Still, both Mrs. Ramsay and Julia remained devoted to their husbands, despite the men's outrageous behaviors."

concern that he is a failure. When the subject of writers comes up during dinner, Mrs. Ramsay monitors the conversation so that it will not upset Mr. Ramsay. She genuinely loves her husband. When she senses the need for him to hear that she loves him, she finds a way to tell him, even though she cannot bring herself to say the words.

Mrs. Ramsay and Julia were heavily involved in the lives of people around them, imparting their Victorian values as they saw fit. Mrs. Ramsay has an uncanny knack for understanding people's emotions. Woolf writes of Mrs. Ramsay,

> Her eyes were so clear that they seemed to go round the table unveiling each of these people, and their thoughts and their feelings, without effort like a light stealing under water.[4]

She uses this ability to guess at her husband's emotions, reading between his words to know what he needs to hear from her. In Woolf's memoirs she identifies this ability to intuit human emotion as one

Argument Four

The author's final argument compares Mrs. Ramsay's and Julia's values and interactions with others: "Mrs. Ramsay and Julia were heavily involved in the lives of people around them, imparting their Victorian values as they saw fit."

her mother also possessed. Julia used this ability to impart Victorian ideals to those around her. Both Mrs. Ramsay and Julia were firm believers in the importance of marriage. Like Mrs. Ramsay, Julia attempted to ensure the tradition of marriage by arranging marriages for people. Julia helped arrange the marriage of her friends the Maxses, though the marriage eventually failed. Mrs. Ramsay set up the marriage of Paul and Minta; however, Lily imagines later on that their marriage also failed.

Conclusion
The conclusion partially restates the thesis and summarizes the main arguments. The conclusion also leaves the reader with a new idea: by basing Mrs. Ramsay on Julia, Woolf gives the character a special depth.

The physical traits, mannerisms, and similar family situations shared by Mrs. Ramsay and Julia indicate that Mrs. Ramsay is a direct portrait of Woolf's mother. Both women suffered from intense sadness and possessed an unwavering devotion to their immature and demanding husbands. Additionally, both women died relatively young, leaving a noticeable absence in their respective families. By basing Mrs. Ramsay on her own mother, Woolf was able to give the character a depth she might not have otherwise had.

Thinking Critically

Now it is your turn to assess the critique. Consider these questions:

1. The thesis states that Mrs. Ramsay is based on Woolf's mother, Julia. Do you agree with the author? Why or why not? Is there other evidence to support the thesis?

2. This critique focuses on the similarities between Julia and Mrs. Ramsay. Are there any differences between the two women?

3. A conclusion should restate the thesis and summarize the arguments. Is this conclusion successful? How could you rewrite the last sentence of the conclusion?

Other Approaches

There are many ways to approach biographical criticism. This essay was only one example of a biographical critique of *To the Lighthouse*. Other critiques might take a closer look at other characters in the novel. One approach might compare Mr. Ramsay to Woolf's father. Another might examine the character Lily and speculate who she might have represented from Woolf's life.

Mr. Ramsay and Mr. Stephen

Leslie Stephen was as obsessed with his work as the character Mr. Ramsay. He fretted over his success as a writer. He constantly fished for compliments about his work. The Stephen siblings were highly critical of their father's self-centered tendencies. They even suggested that the pressure of pleasing their father contributed to their mother's death. An essay could point out the parallels between how the Ramsay and Stephen children reacted to their fathers' behaviors and work obsessions.

A thesis statement for this idea might be: The Ramsay siblings' criticism of Mr. Ramsay mirrors the feelings Woolf and her siblings had for their own father. One argument could show how the character James and his displeasure with his father can be compared to Woolf's younger brother, Adrian's, feelings toward his father, Leslie.

Lily and Woolf

Much like Lily Briscoe, Woolf did not feel she fit the role of the ideal Victorian woman. She found the Victorian expectations for women to be oppressive and unreasonable. Instead of focusing on being the perfect woman, Woolf focused on Lily's writing. She was an unconventional woman for her time. The character Lily in *To The Lighthouse* voices the same opinions about marriage and gender roles that Woolf did. Like Woolf, Lily is also an unconventional woman, but unlike Woolf, Lily never marries and instead devotes herself to painting.

Another possible biographical critique on *To The Lighthouse* could focus on how Lily reflects Woolf's views on womanhood. A thesis for a critique discussing this concept might be: The character Lily in *To The Lighthouse* voices the same opinions about marriage and gender roles Virginia Woolf held.

ADVENTURE PICTURES
Presents
a film by SALLY POTTER
based on the book by VIRGINIA WOOLF

ORLANDO

TILDA SWINTON

ADVENTURE PICTURES
PRESENTS A CO-PRODUCTION WITH
LENFILM MIKADO FILM RIO
SIGMA FILMPRODUCTIONS
WITH THE PARTICIPATION OF
BRITISH SCREEN
DEVELOPED WITH THE SUPPORT OF THE
EUROPEAN SCRIPT FUND
A FILM BY
SALLY POTTER
BASED ON THE BOOK BY
VIRGINIA WOOLF
ORLANDO
TILDA SWINTON
BILLY ZANE
LOTHAIRE BLUTEAU
JOHN WOOD
CHARLOTTE VALANDREY
HEATHCOTE WILLIAMS
AND QUENTIN CRISP
COSTUME DESIGN
SANDY POWELL
PRODUCTION DESIGN
BEN VAN OS JAN ROELFS
MUSIC COMPOSED BY
DAVID MOTION
AND SALLY POTTER
MUSIC SUPERVISOR
BOB LAST
EDITOR
HERVE SCHNEID
DIRECTOR OF PHOTOGRAPHY
ALEXEI RODIONOV
PRODUCED BY
CHRISTOPHER SHEPPARD
WRITTEN & DIRECTED BY
SALLY POTTER

In 1992, a film adaptation of Woolf's novel *Orlando* was released.

9

An Overview of *Orlando*

Orlando is written as a biography of the nobleman Orlando, who is born into a prominent sixteenth-century family. The narrative spans more than 300 years, though Orlando ages only 36 years. He lives through to the twentieth century, changing genders halfway through the novel.

The story begins with Orlando as an attractive 16-year-old boy. Queen Elizabeth has come to visit the area of England in which he lives. She takes an instant liking to him. When Orlando is 18, the Queen sends for him. She gives him a job at the court and falls in love with him. One day, she spies him kissing a young woman and becomes enraged. Orlando begins frequenting pubs at night and spending time with people from the lower classes. He soon tires of them and returns to court. Queen

Elizabeth has died, and he is once again accepted by society. He becomes engaged to a beautiful noblewoman named Euphrosyne.

The Great Frost

When the Great Frost hits England, the entire country is frozen over. The king takes this as an opportunity to have some fun and everyone in London goes ice-skating on the frozen river. While ice-skating, Orlando sees Sasha, a Russian princess, skating extremely well. He is initially not certain whether Sasha is a man or a woman but is nonetheless overwhelmed by his attraction. He sees Sasha curtsy and discovers she is, in fact, a woman.

Sasha does not speak English, but she can speak French. Orlando is the only person who speaks French at court, so Sasha and Orlando become immediately acquainted. They fall in love, though Orlando is still engaged, and plan to run away together. One day, Orlando catches Sasha sitting on the lap of a sailor. Sasha swears it was nothing, and a still-suspicious Orlando chooses to believe her. That same night, he asks her to run away with him. They plan to meet at midnight, but Sasha never arrives. The next day, the ice on the river begins to break up, and Orlando sees the Russian ship sailing off into the distance. He knows Sasha is on it.

Changes

Sasha's betrayal throws Orlando into a bout of depression, and he falls into a trance for seven days. He is exiled from court and locks himself up in his house, where he dedicates himself to writing. By the time he is 25 years old, he has written more than 47 plays, books, and poems. He invites the poet Nick Greene to his house but is disappointed by Greene's bad manners. Greene writes a parody of Orlando, which greatly upsets Orlando and causes him to burn all of his writing except for his poem "The Oak Tree." He works on "The Oak Tree" throughout the rest of the story.

A tall woman, Archduchess Harriet, visits Orlando. Orlando thinks she looks like a hare, but he is suddenly attracted to her. He is repulsed by this attraction because it is lust rather than love. He decides to leave England immediately.

Orlando goes to Constantinople, Turkey, as the English ambassador there. He does such a good job that the king of England makes him a duke. A woman travels from London to be with him, and he receives many letters from women seeking his attention. However, the narrator says, "This romantic power, it is well known, is often associated with a nature of extreme reserve. Orlando seems to have made no friends. As far as is known, he formed no attachments."[1]

On the same night he is made a duke, a washerwoman sees him on his balcony embracing a strange woman. The next morning the servants find him alone and in a trance he cannot be awakened from. A marriage certificate on his desk states that he is married to Rosina Pepita, a Spanish dancer. While he is in the trance, the Turks revolt against the sultan and kill or capture all foreigners. When they find Orlando in a trance, they believe he is dead and leave him alone. On the seventh day of the trance, Orlando wakes up as a woman. He is not surprised by his sex change at all. Orlando is from this point on referred to as "she" instead of "he." She is now 30 years old.

Life as a Woman

Orlando runs away from Constantinople with an old gypsy and lives with gypsies in the mountains of Turkey. However, the gypsies find Orlando's love of nature strange. They become suspicious of her. She soon returns to England.

It is now the eighteenth century. On her way back to England, Orlando grapples with what it means to be a woman. She thinks about how her behavior is different toward men now. She lays out the differences between men and women and how they are treated in society. When she arrives in England, Archduchess Harriet meets her and reveals to Orlando that she is actually a man: Archduke Harry. Archduke Harry confesses that he fell in love with Orlando when he saw a portrait of Orlando as a man. Archduke Harry then dressed as a woman to try to get Orlando to fall in love with him. He professes his undying love for Orlando and asks her to marry him. Orlando does not give him an answer.

Archduke Harry comes to visit Orlando every day for several days in a row. They find they have nothing to talk about, but Archduke Harry's love for Orlando does not waver. To pass the time they bet on where flies will land in the room. Orlando cheats by sticking a fly to a sugar cube. She hopes that when Archduke Harry finds out she cheated, he will be "manly enough" to refuse to marry a dishonest woman.[2] When Archduke Harry discovers her deceit, he bursts into tears but still wants to marry her. Orlando then plays a trick on him by putting a frog down his coat. To Orlando's relief, an enraged Archduke Harry quickly leaves.

Orlando starts spending time with famous poets, but they do not respect her because she is a woman. She begins dressing up as a man and going out at night. One of these nights she meets the prostitute Nell. Thinking Orlando is a man, Nell tries to seduce her and takes her to a rented room. When Orlando admits she is actually a woman, Nell laughs and they become friends. Orlando continues enjoying the benefits of both genders, switching between male and female clothes. One day, Orlando looks up and sees clouds are coming. This marks the beginning of the nineteenth century.

Life in the Present

The Victorian era has begun. Orlando now feels she must find a husband in order to fit in to society. She goes for a walk and breaks her ankle. As she sits and looks out on the landscape, she declares she will be "nature's bride."[3] Just then a man rides by on a horse and asks if she is all right. The man is Marmaduke Bonthrop Shelmerdine, known as Shel.

The two instantly fall madly in love. To Orlando, Shel seems much like a woman and to Shel, Orlando seems much like a man. Shel is a seaman and must go back to sea when the winds change. The couple marries just before Shel departs.

Orlando finally finishes her poem "The Oak Tree." The twentieth century begins, and the world is less gloomy. Orlando gives birth to a son. Several years go by and it is 1928. Orlando is in a store and smells a candle. She feels Sasha's presence. On the way home she thinks about how everything is connected and about all the different lives she has lived. She is now 36 years old.

Orlando begins to be overwhelmed by the present. She thinks about how all things will eventually belong to history. She looks up at the sky and sees an airplane. All of a sudden, her husband, Shel, jumps down from the sky. A clock strikes, and it is midnight.

Orlando begins the novel as a man but changes genders halfway through the story.

How to Apply Gender Criticism to *Orlando*

No.2

What Is Gender Criticism?

Gender criticism's purpose is to question preconceived notions of gender. Gender critics believe gender is socially constructed by the cultures in which people live. They believe men and women are not born any particular way but have been trained to act in typically masculine and feminine ways. Gender criticism suggests men and women learn these behaviors through how society tells them to act. Gender criticism intersects with feminist criticism in its belief that Western civilization is inherently patriarchal.

Some examples of questions a gender critic might ask are: How are men and women expected to behave in this text? Do the characters live up to these expectations or defy them?

Applying Gender Criticism to *Orlando*

Orlando was written during a time of transition for England. In the Victorian era, men and women were expected to follow strict codes of conduct assigned to their genders, but after World War I, gender roles had begun to be more flexible. Still, women were expected to marry, raise families, and see to all domestic responsibilities. In contrast, men were painted as protectors and lawmakers, and they bore the responsibilities of running the world.

As a female writer and women's rights advocate, Woolf was highly critical of these roles. She saw no real difference between the qualities of the male and female intellect, though she noticed a measurable difference in perspective. In *Orlando*, Woolf blurs the line between male and female gender roles with the prominence of androgynous characters, gender-bending behavior, and cross-dressing. The ever-changing gender roles in *Orlando* illustrate the idea that gender is a social construct.

Thesis Statement

The author's thesis statement reads: "The ever-changing gender roles in *Orlando* illustrate the idea that gender is a social construct." The author spends the rest of the essay discussing the way the gender roles portrayed in the novel prove gender is a performance.

<u>Many of the male-female</u>
<u>relationships in *Orlando* defy</u>
<u>traditional social conventions.</u>
In Western society, men are
typically expected to pursue
women in romantic relationships.
However, when Orlando is a
man, women constantly pursue
him. Queen Elizabeth falls in
love with him almost on sight, bringing him into her
court as soon as he is old enough. When Orlando
moves to Turkey, a woman from England moves
there just to be near him and "pestered him with her
attentions."[1] These events break from traditional
gender roles. Many of the women in *Orlando*
are bold in romance. They take the initiative to
approach Orlando almost forcefully. Archduke
Harry goes so far as to disguise his gender to pursue
Orlando. As a man, Orlando only actively pursues
one woman, Sasha, throughout the novel.

During the time the book was written, women
were expected to be submissive to men. Men were
also assumed to be intellectually superior to women.
In *Orlando*, this is not the case. As a woman,
Orlando exercises power in not accepting the

> **Argument One**
> The first argument states:
> "Many of the male-female
> relationships in *Orlando* defy
> traditional social conventions."
> The author opens with a
> general discussion of male-
> female relationships in
> *Orlando*.

Archduke Harry's hand in marriage. She ridicules him by putting a frog in his coat. She also cheats in a betting game, thinking the archduke will be manly enough to reject her after she lies to him. Her cunning proves she is just as intelligent, if not more so, than the archduke. Her boldness in antagonizing him shows she is anything but meek. In contrast to the common stereotype of women being overly emotional, Archduke Harry is the one who ends up in tears. He bursts out crying while confessing his love for Orlando. Orlando, on the other hand, shows no emotional vulnerability to Archduke Harry.

Orlando's relationships with Sasha and Archduke Harry imply attraction has no gender. Orlando feels a strong attraction to Sasha, the Russian princess, without knowing whether she is male or female. Archduke Harry is initially attracted to Orlando, even though he is a man. He dresses as a woman to win Orlando's affections, showing how gender is truly a performance. Archduke Harry thinks if he acts the part of a

> **Argument Two**
> The author now shifts the critique to more closely examine two of Orlando's most prominent relationships. The second argument reads: "Orlando's relationships with Sasha and Archduke Harry imply attraction has no gender."

woman Orlando will believe he is a woman, though biologically he is a man.

Archduke Harry is in love with Orlando whether Orlando is male or female. When Archduke Harry is dressed as Archduchess Harriet, Orlando feels a strong attraction to him. This brings up questions about Orlando's sexuality. He may have been attracted to men when he was still a man, or he may have been attracted to Archduke Harry because he was dressed as a woman and performed the female gender so convincingly. The ambiguity of Orlando's sexuality illustrates the idea that traditional gender roles do not really exist.

Orlando's behavior and how others receive him changes depending on what gender's clothing he is wearing. This is most obvious when Orlando is a woman in eighteenth-century London and takes up the habit of cross-dressing. Nell is submissive and seductive to Orlando when she believes Orlando to be a man, but as soon as she finds out Orlando is a woman she stops trying to impress her and the two establish a friendship.

> **Argument Three**
> The third argument states: "Orlando's behavior and how others receive him changes depending on what gender's clothing he is wearing." The author now discusses the ways others treat Orlando based on his physical appearance.

When Nell is acting the part of the submissive female, she is not acting like herself. She must drop this act to reveal her true self and begin an authentic friendship with Orlando. This indicates that people act a certain way based on preconceived notions of how men and women should act.

When describing Orlando's habit of cross-dressing, the narrator concludes, "[Clothes] change our view of the world and the world's view of us."[2] In the opinion of the narrator, there are few fundamental differences between men and women, but men and women are treated very differently in society. The disparity in this treatment reflects the gender men or women portray based on their clothing and mannerisms.

Orlando has no reaction to her sex change because she feels the same way as a woman as she did as a man. The narrator writes, "Orlando remained precisely as he had been. The change of sex, though it altered their future, did nothing whatever to change their identity."[3] Here, the narrator seems to differentiate between identity and gender,

Argument Four

In the final argument, the author specifically addresses Orlando's sex change. The fourth argument states: "Orlando has no reaction to her sex change because she feels the same way as a woman as she did as a man."

maintaining that one's sense of self has nothing to do with gender or that one has no gender. However, the narrator states that Orlando's sex change will determine her future, showing that gender matters in terms of how one is treated in society. But this distinction further proves that one's thoughts and feelings have no gender. This point is carried out through the rest of the novel. Though Orlando remains biologically female for the rest of the narrative, she frequently dresses and acts as a man. When she finally marries, her choice of partner is

Orlando seems totally indifferent to her gender change when she changes from male to female.

a man, Shel, in whom she sees characteristics of femininity. Accordingly, Shel appreciates Orlando for her masculine characteristics. Although theirs is a male-female union, the gender roles each play are not based on biological gender.

Conclusion

The conclusion is the final paragraph of the essay. The conclusion partially restates the thesis, now backed up by the supporting arguments.

The fluidity of gender in *Orlando* implies that gender is a social construct. Throughout the novel, Orlando engages in many unconventional male-female relationships. Orlando's attraction to both genders implies attraction has no gender. Furthermore, how Orlando acts and how others act toward Orlando changes depending on which gender's clothing he is wearing. Orlando's lack of surprise when his sex changes highlights the idea that the differences between men and women are purely superficial.

Thinking Critically

Now it is your turn to assess the critique. Consider these questions:

1. Do you agree with the author's thesis that the shifting gender roles in *Orlando* illustrate the idea that gender is a social construct? Why or why not?

2. Consider Orlando's relationship with Archduke Harry at the beginning of the novel. What changed between the two characters after Orlando's sex change? What stayed the same?

3. The conclusion of the essay should partially restate the thesis and summarize the supporting arguments. Does this conclusion do a good job of summing up the critique? How could you improve it?

Other Approaches

The previous essay was just one example of an application of gender criticism to Woolf's novel *Orlando*. Look at key points in the book that question gender roles. How do the men in the novel act in comparison to the women? How is their behavior similar or different? An alternate thesis might take a closer look at Orlando's habit of cross-dressing and the way it affects her identity. Another critique could further analyze the relationships between men and women in *Orlando*.

Cross-Dressing

Orlando's identity changes depending on what gender's clothing Orlando wears. One could argue that the prominence of cross-dressing in *Orlando* reflects the author's belief that gender is an act that people put on. One key example is the difference in Nell's behavior toward Orlando when she thinks Orlando is a man compared to when she finds out Orlando is a woman. Other examples of gender being a performance are the differences and similarities in Orlando and Archduke Harry's interactions when Archduke Harry is dressed as a woman as opposed to when he reveals himself to be a man.

A potential thesis for this approach could be: The prominence of cross-dressing in *Orlando* reflects the belief that gender is an act.

Power Between Men and Women

One popular stereotype that gender critics analyze in literature is the idea that men have complete power over women. It can be argued that Orlando's experiences with women as a man and his experiences with men as a woman question men's absolute power over women.

A thesis addressing these ideas might state: Orlando's experiences with women and his experiences as a woman question men's absolute power over women. One argument might consider Orlando's depression when Sasha leaves him.

You Critique It

Now that you have learned about different critical theories and how to apply them to literature, are you ready to perform your own critique? You have read that this type of evaluation can help you look at literature in a new way and make you pay attention to certain issues you may not have otherwise recognized. So, why not use one of the critical theories profiled in this book to consider a fresh take on your favorite book?

First, choose a theory and the book you want to analyze. Remember that the theory is a springboard for asking questions about the work.

Next, write a specific question that relates to the theory you have selected. Then you can form your thesis, which should provide the answer to that question. Your thesis is the most important part of your critique and offers an argument about the work based on the tenets, or beliefs, of the theory you are applying. Recall that the thesis statement typically appears at the very end of the introductory paragraph of your essay. It is usually only one sentence long.

After you have written your thesis, find evidence to back it up. Good places to start are in the work itself or in journals or articles that discuss what other people have said about it. Since you are critiquing a book, you may also want to read about the author's life so you can get a sense of what factors may have affected the creative process. This can be especially useful if working within historical, biographical, or psychological criticism.

Depending on which theory you are applying, you can often find evidence in the book's language, plot, or character development. You should also explore parts of the book that seem to disprove your thesis and create an argument against them. As you do this, you might want to address what other critics have written about the book. Their quotes may help support your claim.

Before you start analyzing a work, think about the different arguments made in this book. Reflect on how evidence supporting the thesis was presented. Did you find that some of the techniques used to back up the arguments were more convincing than others? Try these methods as you prove your thesis in your own critique.

When you are finished writing your critique, read it over carefully. Is your thesis statement understandable? Do the supporting arguments flow logically, with the topic of each paragraph clearly stated? Can you add any information that would present your readers with a stronger argument in favor of your thesis? Were you able to use quotes from the book, as well as from other critics, to enhance your ideas?

Did you see the work in a new light?

Timeline

1882 Adeline Virginia Stephen is born on January 25 in London, England.

1895 Julia Stephen, Virginia's mother, dies after a bout of influenza; Virginia suffers her first significant nervous breakdown.

1922 Jacob's Room is published.

Woolf meets Vita Sackville-West at a dinner party.

1925 Mrs. Dalloway is published.

1927 To The Lighthouse is published.

1928 Orlando is published.

Woolf delivers her lectures on which A Room of One's Own is based.

1929 A Room of One's Own is published.

1939 World War II begins.

1941 On March 28, Woolf drowns herself in the River Ouse.

1904 — Leslie Stephen, Virginia's father, dies of cancer; the Stephen siblings move to Bloomsbury; Virginia publishes a review and an essay in the *Guardian*.

1905 — Virginia begins teaching at Morley College.

1912 — On August 10, Virginia marries Leonard Woolf.

1914 — World War I begins.

1915 — Woolf's first novel, *The Voyage Out*, is published.

1917 — Leonard and Virginia Woolf establish the Hogarth Press.

Glossary

androgyny
Having both male and female characteristics.

aristocrat
Someone who belongs to the upper class.

bipolar disorder
A condition in which a person suffers from severe and rapid mood swings.

chastity
Purity or virginity.

hallucination
A perception, such as a vision or a sound, that is experienced through one's imagination rather than reality.

intuit
To learn or understand by using one's senses and feelings.

materialistic
Placing high value on physical goods and objects.

parody
> A work that humorously mimics or exaggerates
> another work.

patriarchal
> When a society or organization is mostly ruled by men.

preconceive
> To form an opinion before learning about a subject.

protagonist
> The main character of a story.

shell shock
> A post-traumatic stress disorder under wartime
> conditions that causes intense stress.

tyrannical
> Excessively cruel and power hungry.

validation
> To establish worthiness.

Bibliography of Works and Criticism

Important Works

The Voyage Out, 1915

Jacob's Room, 1922

Mrs. Dalloway, 1925

To The Lighthouse, 1927

Orlando, 1928

A Room of One's Own, 1929

The Waves, 1931

Flush, 1933

The Years, 1937

Three Guineas, 1938

Between the Acts, 1941

Critical Discussions

Hill-Miller, Katherine. *From the Lighthouse to Monk's House: A Guide to Virginia Woolf's Literary Landscapes*. London: Gerald Duckworth, 2001. Print.

Hussey, Mark. *Virginia Woolf A to Z: A Comprehensive Reference for Students, Teachers, and Common Readers to Her Life, Work, and Critical Reception*. New York: Facts on File, 1995. Print.

Squier, Susan Merrill. *Virginia Woolf and London: The Sexual Politics of the City*. North Carolina UP, 2011. Print.

Whitworth, Michael. *Virginia Woolf (Authors in Context)*. New York: Oxford UP, 2005. Print.

Resources

Selected Bibliography

Lee, Hermione. *Virginia Woolf*. New York: Knopf, 1996.
Print.

Overy, Richard. *The Twilight Years: The Paradox of
Britain Between Wars*. New York: Viking Penguin,
2009. Print.

Woolf, Virginia. *Mrs. Dalloway*. Orlando, FL: Harcourt,
1997. Print.

Woolf, Virginia. *To the Lighthouse*. Orlando, FL:
Harcourt, 2005. Print.

Further Readings

Goldman, Jane. *The Cambridge Introduction to Virginia
Woolf*. New York: Cambridge UP, 2006. Print.

Webb, Ruth. *Virginia Woolf*. New York: Oxford UP,
2000. Print.

Woolf, Virginia. *Jacob's Room*. Orlando, FL: Harcourt,
2008. Print.

Web Links

To learn more about critiquing the works of Virginia
Woolf, visit ABDO Publishing Company online at
www.abdopublishing.com. Web sites about the works
of Virginia Woolf are featured on our Book Links page.
These links are routinely monitored and updated to
provide the most current information available.

For More Information

The Modernist Studies Association

Johns Hopkins University, 3400 North Charles Street

Baltimore, MD 21218

1-800-548-1784

msa.press.jhu.edu

The Modernist Studies Association contributes new
information to the study of modernism.

Victoria University Library, University of Toronto

71 Queen's Park Crescent East

Toronto, Ontario, Canada, M5S 1K7

416-585-4470

www.library.vicu.utoronto.ca/index.htm

The Victoria University Library has links to Leonard and
Virginia Woolf's library, an online exhibition of Virginia
Woolf's books and commentaries on her works.

Source Notes

Chapter 1. Introduction to Critiques
None.

Chapter 2. A Closer Look at Virginia Woolf
None.

Chapter 3. An Overview of *Mrs. Dalloway*
1. Virginia Woolf. *Mrs. Dalloway*. New York: Oxford UP, 2000. Print. 50.

Chapter 4. How to Apply Historical Criticism to *Mrs. Dalloway*
1. Virginia Woolf. *Mrs. Dalloway*. New York: Oxford UP, 2000. Print. 20.

2. Ibid. 127.

3. Ibid. 99.

4. Ibid. 49.

5. Ibid. 50.

Chapter 5. An Overview of *A Room of One's Own*

    1. Virginia Woolf. *A Room of One's Own*. Orlando,
FL: Harcourt, 2005. Print. 4.

    2. Ibid. 8.

    3. Ibid. 78.

**Chapter 6. How to Apply Feminist Criticism
to *A Room of One's Own***

    1. Virginia Woolf. *A Room of One's Own*. Orlando,
FL: Harcourt, 2005. Print. 29.

    2. Ibid. 63–64.

Chapter 7. An Overview of *To the Lighthouse*
None.

Chapter 8. How to Apply Biographical Criticism to *To the Lighthouse*

1. Katherine Dalsimer. *Virginia Woolf.* New Haven, CT: Yale UP, 2001. Print. 115.

2. Hermione Lee. *Virginia Woolf.* New York: Knopf, 1996. Print. 93.

3. Virginia Woolf. *To the Lighthouse*. Orlando, FL: Harcourt, 1989. Print. 32.

4. Ibid. 106.

Chapter 9. An Overview of *Orlando*

1. Virginia Woolf. *Orlando*. Orlando, FL: Harcourt, 2006. Print. 92.

2. Ibid. 135.

3. Ibid. 182.

Chapter 10. How to Apply Gender Criticism to *Orlando*

1. Virginia Woolf. *Orlando*. Orlando, FL: Harcourt, 2006. Print. 92.

2. Ibid. 138.

3. Ibid. 102.

Index

About the Author

Rosa Boshier is a freelance writer, artist, and educator. She lives in California.

Photo Credits